I0006238

Understanding Your Laptop as a Beginner

Mastering the Basics of Computing and Unleashing the Full Potential of Your Laptop

By

John George

Dedication

In this guide, we'll cover everything from choosing the right laptop for your needs to setting up your email and social media accounts. We'll also walk you through the process of installing antivirus software and other essential applications. Additionally, we'll provide tips on how to keep your laptop running smoothly, including how to clean it and optimize its performance.

One of the most important steps in setting up your laptop is choosing the right operating system. Whether you prefer Windows, macOS, or Linux, we'll provide you with an overview of each operating system's features and benefits. We'll also walk you through the process of installing your chosen operating system and configuring it to your liking.

Once your operating system is installed, we'll help you set up your user account and configure your settings. From there, we'll guide you through the process of installing essential software such as Microsoft Office, Adobe Creative Suite, and other productivity tools.

We'll also show you how to set up your email and social media accounts, including Gmail, Outlook, Facebook, Twitter, and more. Additionally, we'll provide tips on how to keep your accounts secure and protect your personal information.

Finally, we'll provide tips on how to keep your laptop running smoothly and efficiently. This includes everything from cleaning your keyboard and screen to optimizing your battery life and managing your storage space.

Whether you're a student, professional, or casual user, this guide is designed to help you get the most out of your laptop. With clear and concise instructions, you'll be able to set up and use your device with confidence. So let's begin on this exciting journey together!

Introduction

This guide provides a comprehensive overview of how to set up and optimize your laptop for your needs. It covers everything from choosing the right operating system to installing essential software and setting up your email and social media accounts.

Additionally, it provides tips on how to keep your laptop running smoothly and efficiently. Whether you're a student, professional, or casual user, this guide will help you get the most out of your device.

Table of contents

Chapter 1. Unboxing and setting up the laptop.

Chapter I of this guide is an essential starting point for anyone who has just purchased a new laptop and wants to set it up. The chapter provides a step-by-step guide for unboxing the laptop, connecting the charger, and turning on the laptop for the first time.

The first step in setting up a new laptop is to unbox it carefully. This involves removing all the packaging materials, including the plastic wrap, cardboard box, and any other protective materials. It is important to take care when removing these materials to avoid damaging the laptop.

Once the laptop is out of the box, the next step is to connect the charger. This involves finding the power cord and plugging it into the laptop's charging port. It is important to ensure that the charger is properly connected before attempting to turn on the laptop.

After connecting the charger, the next step is to turn on the laptop for the first time. This involves pressing the power button, which is usually located on the side or front of the laptop. Once the laptop is turned on, it will begin to boot up, which may take several minutes.

As the laptop boots up, it may prompt the user to enter some basic information such as their name, language preference, and time zone. It is important to follow these prompts carefully to ensure that the laptop is set up correctly.

Once the laptop is fully booted up and ready to use, the user can begin to explore its features and settings. This may include setting up a user account, connecting to Wi-Fi, and installing any necessary software or updates.

When you first receive your laptop, it is important to connect the charger and turn it on properly to ensure that it works correctly and to avoid any damage.

To connect the charger, locate the charging port on your laptop. It is usually located on the side or back of the device and is typically marked with a small icon that looks like a battery. Once you have located the charging port, plug the charger into the port and then plug the other end into a power outlet.

After connecting the charger, you can turn on your laptop for the first time. To do this, locate the power button on your device. The power button is usually located on the top row of keys on your keyboard and is marked with a small icon that looks like a circle with a line through it. Press and hold down the power button for a few seconds until you see the screen light up.

Once your laptop has turned on, you may be prompted to enter some basic information such as your language preference and Wi-Fi network details. Follow the prompts to complete the setup process and then you are ready to start using your new laptop.

It is important to note that when connecting the charger and turning on your laptop for the first time, you should always follow the manufacturer's instructions. If you are unsure about any aspect of the setup process, consult the user manual or contact customer support for assistance.

Overall, Chapter I of this guide provides a comprehensive and easy-to-follow guide for setting up a new laptop. By following these steps carefully, even beginners can quickly and easily get their laptop up and running without any hassle.

Chapter 2: Customizing Your Laptop

After setting up your new laptop, the next step is to customize it to your liking. Chapter 2 of this guide provides a step-by-step guide for personalizing your laptop's settings and features.

The first step in customizing your laptop is to set up a user account. This involves creating a username and password that will be used to log in to the laptop. It is advice to choose a strong password that is difficult for others to guess or manipulate.

Once the user account is set up, the next step is to personalize the laptop's desktop background and theme. This can be done by selecting a pre-installed background or by uploading a custom image. The theme can also be changed to suit your preferences.

After customizing the desktop, the next step is to configure the laptop's settings. This includes adjusting the display settings, sound settings, and power settings. It is important to adjust these settings to optimize the laptop's performance and battery life.

Another important aspect of customizing your laptop is installing software and applications that you need. This may include productivity tools, entertainment apps, or antivirus software. It is important to only install software from trusted sources to avoid malware and other security issues.

In addition to software, you may also want to customize the laptop's hardware. This includes adding peripherals such as a mouse or external hard drive. It may also involve upgrading the laptop's RAM or hard drive for better performance.

Tips

Customizing your new laptop is an important step in making it work for you. There are several ways to customize your laptop, including changing the desktop background, installing software, and adjusting settings.

One of the first things you may want to do is change the desktop background. This can be done by right-clicking on the desktop and selecting "Personalize" or "Display Settings" depending on your operating system. From there, you can choose a pre-installed background or upload your own image.

Next, you may want to install software that you frequently use. This can include productivity tools, media players, or games. You can download and install software from the internet or use a pre-installed app store.

Adjusting settings is another way to customize your laptop. This can include changing the language, adjusting the screen resolution, or changing the power settings. To access these settings, navigate to the control panel or settings app on your device.

It is important to note that while customizing your laptop can make it work better for you, it is also important to be cautious about what you install and change. Installing too many programs or changing too many settings can slow down your device and potentially cause issues.

Customizing your new laptop is a great way to make it work for you and improve your overall experience. Just be sure to do so carefully and with consideration for the impact on your device's performance.

This guide provides a comprehensive guide for customizing your new laptop. By following these steps, you can make your laptop truly your own and optimize its performance for your needs.

Chapter 3: Maintaining Your Laptop

After customizing your laptop, it is important to maintain it to ensure optimal performance and longevity. Chapter 3 of this guide provides a step-by-step guide for maintaining your laptop.

The first step in maintaining your laptop is to keep it clean. This involves wiping down the screen and keyboard regularly with a microfiber cloth and using compressed air to remove dust and debris from the vents. It is also important to avoid eating or drinking near the laptop to prevent spills.

Another important aspect of maintaining your laptop is updating the software and drivers. This ensures that the laptop is running the latest security patches and bug fixes. It is recommended to set up automatic updates to ensure that the laptop stays up-to-date.

In addition to software updates, it is important to keep the laptop's hardware in good condition. This includes checking the battery health and replacing it if necessary. It also involves monitoring the laptop's temperature to prevent overheating.

Backing up important files is another crucial aspect of maintaining your laptop. This involves regularly backing up files to an external hard drive or cloud storage service to prevent data loss in case of hardware failure or other issues.

Finally, it is important to address any issues promptly. This includes troubleshooting common problems such as slow performance, connectivity issues, or software crashes. It may also involve seeking professional help for more complex issues.

Tips

Maintaining a new laptop is essential to ensure its longevity and optimal performance. Here are some tips for maintaining your new laptop:

1. Keep it clean: Regularly clean your laptop's keyboard, touchpad, and screen with a soft cloth. Avoid using harsh chemicals or abrasive materials that can damage the surface.

2. Protect it: Use a laptop case or sleeve to protect your device from scratches, spills, and other potential damage.

3. Keep it cool: Overheating can cause damage to your laptop's hardware, so make sure to keep it cool by placing it on a flat surface and avoiding blocking the vents.

4. Update software: Keep your operating system and other software up to date to ensure security and performance improvements.

5. Back up data: Regularly back up your important files and documents to an external hard drive or cloud storage to prevent loss in case of a malfunction or theft.

6. Use antivirus software: Install antivirus software to protect your laptop from viruses, malware, and other online threats.

7. Uninstall unused programs: Remove any programs or apps that you no longer use to free up space and improve performance.

By following these maintenance tips, you can ensure that your new laptop remains in good condition and provides you with optimal performance for years to come.

Chapter 4: Protecting Your Laptop

In today's digital age, protecting your laptop from cyber threats is more important than ever. Chapter 4 of this guide provides a step-by-step guide for protecting your laptop from malware, viruses, and other cyber threats.

The first step in protecting your laptop is to install reputable antivirus software. This software can detect and remove malicious software that may harm your laptop or compromise your personal information. It is important to keep the antivirus software up-to-date to ensure optimal protection.

Another important aspect of protecting your laptop is to secure your internet connection. This includes using a strong and unique password for your Wi-Fi network and avoiding public Wi-Fi networks that may be vulnerable to cyber attacks.

It is also important to practice safe browsing habits when using the internet. This includes avoiding suspicious websites and links, and being cautious when downloading files or opening email attachments.

In addition to these measures, it is recommended to use a virtual private network (VPN) to encrypt your internet traffic and protect your online privacy. This is especially important when using public Wi-Fi networks or accessing sensitive information online.

Protecting a new laptop is crucial to ensure its longevity and optimal performance. One of the most effective ways to protect your laptop is by using a laptop case or sleeve. These protective covers are designed to shield your laptop from scratches, spills, and other potential damage. They come in various sizes and materials, including neoprene, leather, and hard shell cases.

Another way to protect your laptop is by keeping it cool. Overheating can cause damage to your laptop's hardware, so make sure to place it on a flat surface and avoid blocking the vents. You can also use a cooling pad or a laptop stand with built-in fans to improve airflow and reduce heat.

In addition, it's essential to keep your laptop safe from theft or loss. You can do this by using a laptop lock or a security cable to secure your device to a desk or other fixed object. You can also enable the built-in security features of your laptop, such as password protection, fingerprint recognition, or facial recognition.

Moreover, it's crucial to back up your data regularly to prevent loss in case of a malfunction or theft. You can use an external hard drive or cloud storage to store your important files and documents securely.

Installing antivirus software is another crucial step in protecting your new laptop. Antivirus software can detect and remove viruses, malware, and other online threats that can compromise your security and privacy.

Protecting a new laptop requires a combination of physical protection, security measures, and data backup. By following these tips, you can ensure that your laptop remains in good condition and provides you with optimal performance for years to come.

Finally, it is important to back up your data regularly to prevent data loss in case of a cyber attack or hardware failure. This involves regularly backing up files to an external hard drive or cloud storage service.

Chapter 5: Maintaining Your Laptop

Maintaining your laptop is essential to ensure that it runs smoothly and efficiently. Chapter 5 of this guide provides a step-by-step guide for maintaining your laptop and prolonging its lifespan.

The first step in maintaining your laptop is to keep it clean. This involves regularly wiping down the screen and keyboard with a microfiber cloth and using compressed air to remove dust and debris from the vents and ports.

Another important aspect of maintaining your laptop is to keep it updated. This includes installing software updates and security patches, as well as updating drivers and firmware. This ensures that your laptop is running the latest software and is protected from security vulnerabilities.

It is also important to manage your laptop's storage space. This involves regularly deleting unnecessary files and programs, and using a disk cleanup tool to free up space. This can help improve your laptop's performance and prevent it from slowing down.

Apart from the tips mentioned above, there are several other ways to maintain your new laptop and prevent it from getting damaged. Here are some additional tips:

1. Keep your laptop clean: Dust and dirt can accumulate on your laptop's surface and vents, which can cause overheating and hardware damage.

Use a soft cloth or microfiber towel to wipe your laptop regularly. Always make use of compressed air to blow out any dust or debris from the vents.

2. Avoid eating or drinking near your laptop: Spills can cause serious damage to your laptop's keyboard, motherboard, and other components. Keep food and drinks away from your laptop, and if you must eat or drink, use a spill-proof container.

3. Be careful with the power cord: The power cord is one of the most vulnerable parts of your laptop. Avoid pulling or twisting the cord, and never wrap it tightly around your laptop. Also, make sure to unplug the cord when not in use.

4. Don't overload your laptop: Running too many programs or applications simultaneously can put a strain on your laptop's hardware and cause it to slow down or freeze. Close any unnecessary programs and limit the number of browser tabs you have open.

5. Keep your laptop up-to-date: Regularly update your operating system, drivers, and software to ensure that your laptop is running smoothly and securely. Bug fixes, security patches, and performance enhancements are frequently included in updates.

By following these tips, you can maintain your new laptop and prevent it from getting damaged. Remember to treat your laptop with care and respect, and it will serve you well for years to come.

In addition to these measures, it is recommended to optimize your laptop's power settings. This includes adjusting the screen brightness, turning off unused features, and using a power-saving mode to conserve battery life.

Chapter 6: Securing Your Laptop

Maintaining your laptop is crucial to ensure that it continues to perform at its best. Chapter 7 of this guide provides tips and guidelines for maintaining your laptop and keeping it in good condition.

1. Keep it clean: Regularly clean your laptop's keyboard, screen, and case with a soft cloth or microfiber cloth. Abrasive or harsh chemicals should not be used as they can harm the surface.

2. Update software: Keep your operating system and software up to date to ensure that your laptop is protected from security vulnerabilities and runs smoothly.

3. Remove unused programs: Uninstall any programs or apps that you no longer use to free up space on your hard drive and improve performance.

4. Use antivirus software: Install and regularly update antivirus software to protect your laptop from malware and viruses.

5. Manage power settings: Adjust the power settings to optimize battery life and reduce energy consumption when using your laptop on battery power.

6. Keep it cool: Overheating can cause damage to your laptop's components, so make sure that it has proper ventilation and avoid using it on soft surfaces like beds or couches that can block air flow.

7. Backup data regularly: Regularly backup important files and data to an external hard drive or cloud storage service to prevent data loss in case of a hardware failure or other issues.

By following these tips and guidelines, you can maintain your laptop's performance and prolong its lifespan. Regular maintenance can also save you money in the long run by preventing costly repairs or replacements.

It is important to monitor your laptop's performance and troubleshoot any issues that may arise. This involves running diagnostic tests, checking for hardware errors, and seeking professional help if necessary.

Securing your new laptop from theft is just as important as maintaining its physical condition.

Here are some tips to keep your laptop safe from theft:

1. Use a strong password: Set up a strong password that is difficult to guess or crack. Avoid using common words, dates, or personal information that can be easily guessed.

2. Enable two-factor authentication: Two-factor authentication adds an extra layer of security to your login process. This requires you to enter a unique code sent to your phone or email before you can access your account.

3. Install anti-theft software: Anti-theft software can help you track and recover your laptop if it is stolen. Some popular options include Prey, LoJack, and Find My Device.

4. Use a cable lock: A cable lock is a physical security device that attaches to your laptop and locks it to a stationary object, such as a desk or table. This can prevent someone from stealing your laptop when you are away from it.

5. Be aware of your surroundings: When using your laptop in public places, be aware of your

surroundings and keep an eye on your laptop at all times. Avoid leaving it unattended or in plain sight.

6. Backup your data: In case your laptop is stolen, make sure to backup your important data regularly. This can help you recover your files even if you cannot recover your laptop.

This guide provides a comprehensive guide for maintaining your laptop and keeping it running smoothly. By following these steps, you can prolong the lifespan of your laptop and ensure that it continues to meet your needs for years to come.

By following these tips, you can secure your new laptop from theft and ensure that your personal information and data are protected. Remember to always be vigilant and take precautions to keep your laptop safe.

Chapter 7: Upgrading Your Laptop

As technology advances, it is important to keep your laptop up to date in order to keep up with the latest software and hardware requirements. Chapter 6 of this guide provides a step-by-step guide for upgrading your laptop and improving its performance.

The first step in upgrading your laptop is to determine what needs to be upgraded. This can include upgrading the RAM, hard drive, or processor. It is important to research the specific requirements for your laptop and ensure that any upgrades are compatible.

Once you have determined what needs to be upgraded, the next step is to purchase the necessary components. This may involve purchasing new RAM modules, a larger hard drive, or a faster processor. It is important to purchase high-quality components from reputable manufacturers in order to ensure compatibility and reliability.

Before beginning the upgrade process, it is important to back up all of your important data and files. An external hard drive or cloud storage platform can be used for this. By doing this, you can be sure that your data is secure in the event that something goes wrong with the upgrade. The actual upgrade process will vary depending on what components are being upgraded. It is important to follow the manufacturer's instructions carefully and to take precautions such as grounding yourself to prevent static electricity damage.

Once the upgrade is complete, it is important to test the laptop to ensure that everything is working properly. This may involve running diagnostic tests or benchmarking software to measure the performance improvements.

How to upgrade ur new laptop tips

Upgrading your new laptop can help improve its performance and extend its lifespan.

Some tips on how to upgrade your laptop:

1. Upgrade the RAM: Upgrading the RAM can help improve the speed and performance of your laptop. Check the maximum amount of RAM your laptop can support and purchase the appropriate RAM module.

2. Upgrade the hard drive: Upgrading the hard drive can help increase storage capacity and improve overall performance. Consider upgrading to a solid-state drive (SSD) for faster read and write speeds.

3. Upgrade the graphics card: If you use your laptop for gaming or graphic-intensive tasks, consider upgrading the graphics card for better performance.

4. Clean up your system: Regularly clean up your system by removing unnecessary files, programs, and applications. It can also help to free up space and improve performance.

5. Update software and drivers: Make sure to regularly update your software and drivers to ensure that your laptop is running smoothly and securely.

6. Install a cooling pad: If your laptop tends to overheat, consider installing a cooling pad to help regulate the temperature and prevent damage to your laptop.

By following these tips, you can upgrade your new laptop and improve its performance and functionality. Remember to always research and consult with a professional before making any upgrades to ensure compatibility and avoid damaging your laptop.

Chapter 8. Troubleshooting common issues

Troubleshooting common issues for your new laptop can help you identify and resolve any problems that may arise. Here are some tips on how to troubleshoot common issues:

1. Slow Performance: If your laptop is running slow, try closing unnecessary programs and applications, running a virus scan, and clearing temporary files. If the issue persists, consider upgrading the RAM or hard drive as mentioned above.

2. Battery Life: If your laptop's battery life is short, try adjusting the power settings to conserve energy, closing unnecessary programs and applications, and reducing screen brightness. If the issue persists, consider replacing the battery or purchasing a new one.

3. Overheating: If your laptop is overheating, try using a cooling pad, cleaning the vents and fans, and avoiding using the laptop on soft surfaces that block airflow. If the issue persists, consider upgrading the cooling system or consulting with a professional.

4. Wi-Fi Connectivity: If your laptop is having trouble connecting to Wi-Fi, try resetting the router, checking for updates and drivers, and ensuring that the Wi-Fi adapter is turned on. If the issue persists, consider resetting the network settings or consulting with a professional.

5. Blue Screen of Death: If your laptop encounters a blue screen of death (BSOD), try restarting the laptop, checking for updates and drivers, and running a virus scan. If the issue persists, consider restoring the laptop to an earlier date or consulting with a professional.

By following these troubleshooting tips, you can identify and resolve common issues with your new laptop. Remember to always research and consult with a professional before making any changes to avoid damaging your laptop.

Fixing software errors and crashes

Fixing software errors and crashes can be a bit more complicated than other common issues. Here are some steps you can take to troubleshoot and fix software errors and crashes:

1. Identify the Error: When a software error or crash occurs, take note of any error messages or codes that appear. This can help you identify the cause of the issue.

2. Restart the Program: Try restarting the program that is causing the error or crash. This may resolve the issue if it was caused by a temporary glitch.

3. Update Software: Check for any available updates for the program and install them. Updates often include bug fixes and improvements that can resolve errors and crashes.

4. Reinstall Software: If updating the software doesn't work, try uninstalling and reinstalling it. This can replace any corrupted files that may be causing the issue.

5. Scan for Malware: Run a virus scan to check for any malware or viruses that may be causing the error or crash.

6. Check Hardware: Sometimes software errors and crashes can be caused by hardware issues such as a failing hard drive or faulty RAM. Run hardware diagnostics to check for any issues.

7. Consult with a Professional: If the issue persists after trying these steps, it may be necessary to consult with a professional for further assistance.

By following these steps, you can troubleshoot and fix software errors and crashes on your laptop. Remember to always back up important data before making any changes to avoid losing data.

Chapter 9: Conclusion and next steps

In Conclusion

Fixing software errors and crashes can be a bit more complicated than other common issues. Here are some steps you can take to troubleshoot and fix software errors and crashes:

1. Identify the Error: When a software error or crash occurs, take note of any error messages or codes that appear. This can help you identify the cause of the issue.

2. Restart the Program: Try restarting the program that is causing the error or crash. This may resolve the issue if it was caused by a temporary glitch.

3. Update Software: Check for any available updates for the program and install them. Updates often include bug fixes and improvements that can resolve errors and crashes.

4. Reinstall Software: If updating the software doesn't work, try uninstalling and reinstalling it. This can replace any corrupted files that may be causing the issue.

5. Scan for Malware: Run a virus scan to check for any malware or viruses that may be causing the error or crash.

6. Check Hardware: Sometimes software errors and crashes can be caused by hardware issues such as a failing hard drive or faulty RAM. Run hardware diagnostics to check for any issues.

7. Consult with a Professional: If the issue persists after trying these steps, it may be necessary to consult with a professional for further assistance.

By following these steps, you can troubleshoot and fix software errors and crashes on your laptop. Remember to always back up important data before making any changes to avoid losing data.